Sci
Vocabulary Readers

Dolphins

Justin McCory Martin

SCHOLASTIC INC.

NEW YORK • TORONTO • LONDON • AUCKLAND • SYDNEY
MEXICO CITY • NEW DELHI • HONG KONG • BUENOS AIRES

ISBN-13: 978-0-545-00743-6 / ISBN-10: 0-545-00743-7

Photos Credits:
Cover: © Mike Hill/Getty Images; title page: © Todd Pusser/npl/Minden Pictures; contents page, from top: © Konrad Wothe/Minden Pictures, © Jeff Rotman/Nature Picture Library, © Flip Nicklin/Getty Images, © Masa Ushioda/Image Quest Marine; page 4: © Konrad Wothe/Minden Pictures; page 5, top left: © Gerard Lacz/Animals Animals; page 5, top right: © ZSSD/Minden Pictures; page 5, bottom left: © Andy Rouse/Getty Images; page 5, bottom right: © Mel Yates/Getty Images; page 6: © Stephen Frink/Getty Images; page 7: © Stuart Gregory/Getty Images; page 7, inset: © F. Stuart Westmorland/Photo Researchers; page 8: © Jeff Rotman/Nature Picture Library; page 9: © Peter Weimann/Animals Animals; page 10: © VEER Elan Sun Star/Getty Images; page 11: © Flip Nicklin/Minden Pictures; page 11, inset: © Norbert Wu/Minden Pictures; page 12: © Stephen Frink/Getty Images; page 13: © Doug Perrine/Nature Picture Library; page 14: © Flip Nicklin/Getty Images; page 15: © Conrad Wothe/Minden Pictures; page 16, from top: © James Watt/Animals Animals; © Albert Gea/Reuters/Corbis; page 17: © Stuart Westmorland/Getty Images; page 18: © Daniel Ballioti/Animals Animals; page 19: © P. Wegner/Peter Arnold Inc.; page 19, inset: © Car Culture/Corbis; page 20: © Masa Ushioda/Image Quest Marine; page 21: © Flip Nicklin/ Minden Pictures; page 21, inset: © Jeff Rotman/Getty Images; page 22: © Todd Pusser/npl/Minden Pictures; page 24: © Flip Nicklin/Minden Pictures; back cover: © Brandon Cole/Marine Photography/Getty Images.

Photo research by Dwayne Howard
Design by Holly Grundon

12 11 10 9 8 7 6 5 4 3 2 8 9 10 11 12 13/0

Printed in the U.S.A.
First printing, April 2008

Contents

Chapter 1

Meet the Dolphin

bottlenose dolphins

Can dolphins fly? No. But they can leap very high in the air! Let's learn all about these amazing animals of the sea.

dolphin

tiger

gorilla

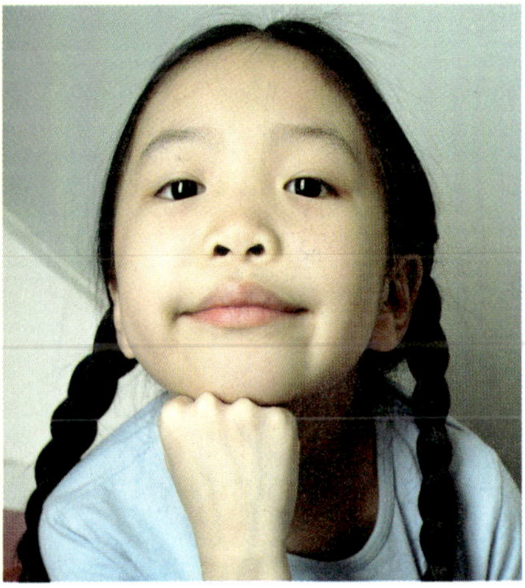

girl

Dolphins live in the water. But they are not fish. They are mammals, just like tigers, gorillas, and people.

Dolphin Parts

Fast Fact

Dolphins have been around for more than 50 million years.

This is a dolphin. Dolphins have a **dorsal fin** and two flippers. Their tail ends in two **flukes**. Dolphins move their tails up and down to swim.

A dolphin's blowhole looks like this close up.

Dolphins have a **beak** filled with razor-sharp teeth. They also have a **blowhole** for breathing air. Dolphins hold their breath underwater.

Chapter 2

Skills and Senses

bottlenose dolphins

Fast Fact

Dolphins can swim about 25 miles per hour.

Dolphins have lots of special skills. For one thing, they are great swimmers. They can swim three times faster than the fastest human.

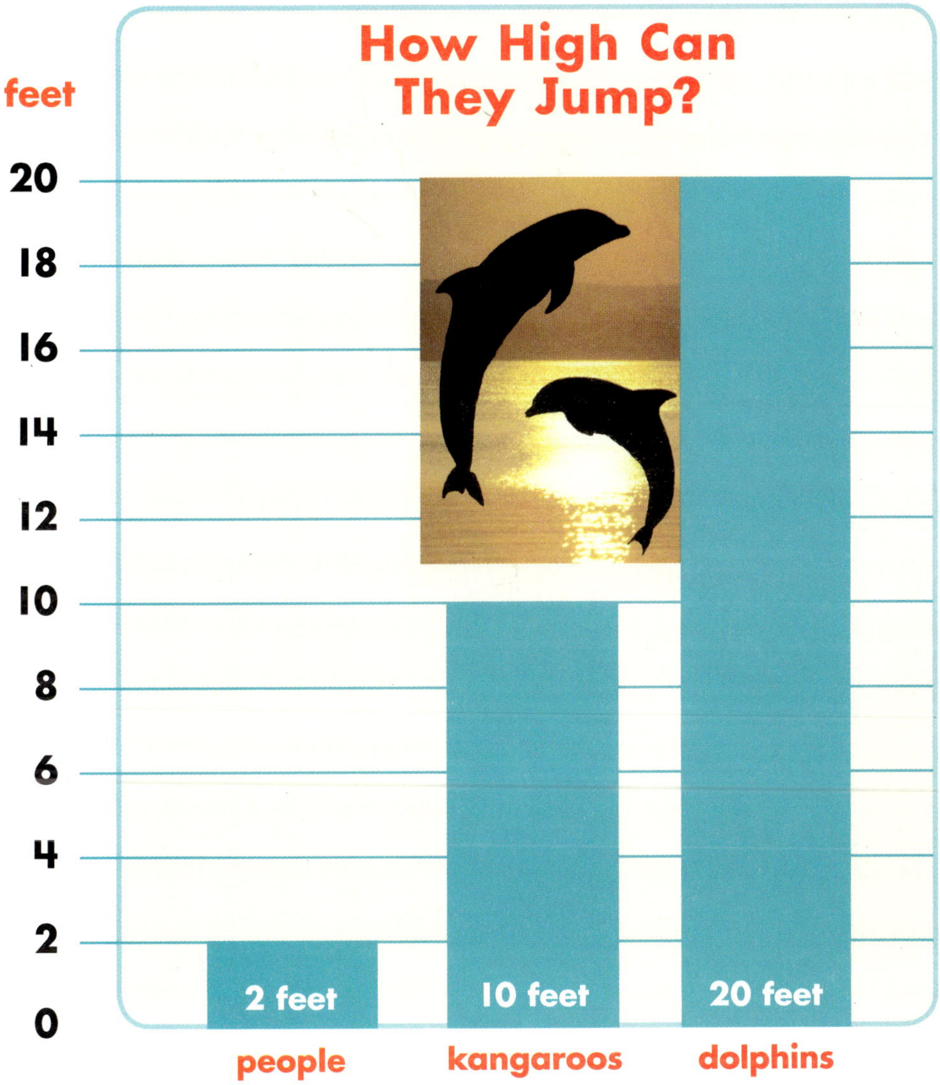

Dolphins are great jumpers, too. They can leap 20 feet in the air. Wow! That is as high as a house.

A man meets a friendly dolphin.

Dolphins are smart and friendly. Sometimes they swim right up to boats. There are even stories about dolphins rescuing swimmers in trouble.

Three bottlenose dolphins play in the water.

spotted Atlantic dolphin

Fast Fact

Dolphins like to play with seaweed.

Dolphins are very playful. They **frolic** together in the water. They blow bubbles. They even play games like catch!

bottlenose dolphin

Dolphins also have a special sense called **echolocation**. First, they make sounds like clicks and squeaks and gurgles. Then they listen for the underwater echoes.

Dolphin Menu

- fish
- squid
- octopus
- shrimp

The echoes tell dolphins the size of nearby sea creatures and their **exact** location. What happens next? The dolphins swim over and find a tasty meal!

Chapter 3

Dolphin Pods

This is a bottlenose dolphin pod.

Dolphins live together in groups called **pods**. A pod usually has one male dolphin called a bull and several females called cows. There are babies, too. They are called calves.

Fast Fact

There can be five to 25 dolphins in a pod.

Two bottlenose dolphins bump heads.

The dolphin pods swim, hunt, and play together. Dolphins communicate with one another by whistling, slapping the water, or bumping heads.

A spotted Atlantic dolphin **nurses** her calf.

A bottlenose dolphin swims with her calf.

Dolphin mothers take good care of their baby calves. They give their calves milk. They teach their calves about the ocean.

A bottlenose dolphin shows her calf how to jump.

Fast Fact

Dolphin calves stay with their mothers for up to six years.

Dolphin mothers show their calves how to dive. They also show their calves how to leap high in the air. Amazing!

Chapter 4

So Many Dolphins

bottlenose dolphins

These are bottlenose dolphins. They are trained to put on shows at **aquariums**. But there are 36 other kinds of dolphins. Let's meet a few.

Fast Fact

Killer whales are also called orcas. They can weigh as much as three cars!

Many people call this a killer whale. But it is really a dolphin. Killer whales are black and white and very big. How big? Some weigh more than 12,000 pounds!

Fast Fact

Commerson's dolphins have two special skills. They can spin while swimming. They can also swim upside-down!

Here is another one. It is called a Commerson's dolphin. It has markings that are the opposite of a killer whale. Cool!

Fast Fact

This dolphin lives in the Amazon River in Brazil.

This is a river dolphin. It lives in the **freshwater** of a river instead of the saltwater of an ocean. River dolphins use their long beaks to poke around and search for food.

Hector's dolphin

Some dolphins are **endangered**. There are less than 4,000 Hector's dolphins left. We must be careful not to harm dolphins. The world would not be complete without these amazing mammals!

Glossary

aquarium (uh-**kwair**-ee-uhm): a zoo-like place where people can go to see marine mammals and fish

beak (**beek**): the snout of a dolphin

blowhole (**bloh**-hohl): a hole for breathing

dorsal fin (**door**-sal **fin**): the fin on a dolphin's back

echolocation (ek-oh-loh-**kay**-shuhn): a special sense in which echoes are used to locate objects

endangered (en-**dayn**-jured): an animal in danger of becoming extinct

exact (eg-**zakt**): perfectly correct

fluke (**flook**): part of a dolphin's tail

freshwater (**fresh**-wa-tur): water that does not contain salt, as in rivers

frolic (**fro**-lik): to play happily

nurse (**nurss**): when a mother gives a baby milk from her body

pod (**pod**): a small herd of marine mammals

Comprehension Questions

1. Can you name three dolphin parts?

2. Can you name three special dolphin skills?

3. Can you name three kinds of dolphins?

4. Can you think of three great words to describe a dolphin?

Bonus Fast Facts

- Some dolphins live to be 50 years old.
- Dolphins use their teeth to catch prey, but not to chew. Dolphins swallow their meals whole.
- Dolphins are sometimes called porpoises. But that is wrong. Porpoises are a different kind of sea mammal.